FOLENS One-a-Week Spell Tests BOOK 2

Guided Activities plus Answers

Rita Ray

Folens Publishers

Editor: Michael Spilling   Cover illustration: Patricia Murray – Graham-Cameron Illustrations
Layout artist: Patricia Hollingsworth   Illustrations: Claire Boyce – Graham-Cameron Illustrations

© 1997 Folens Limited, on behalf of the author.

Every effort has been made to contact copyright holders of material used in this book. If any have been overlooked, we will be pleased to make any necessary arrangements.

British Library Cataloguing in Publication Data. A catalogue record for this book is available from the British Library.

First published 1997 by Folens Limited, Dunstable and Dublin.
Folens Limited, Albert House, Apex Business Centre, Boscombe Road, Dunstable, LU5 4RL, England.

ISBN 1 86202 500-2

Printed in Singapore by Craft Print.

Introduction

One-a-Week Spelling Tests provide a graded set of practice exercises and tests to build up spelling skills. The words have been selected from research into words most used by children at particular stages.

The words are arranged in small groups, which can be focused upon and tested periodically. The units contain key sight words and words with common spelling patterns. In books 1–4, words with similar spelling patterns are presented together and tested in separate sentences. In books 5 and 6, similar spelling patterns are spread throughout the books so that they can be tested in the context of whole passages. This provides a suitable preparation for the format of national tests.

The sentences used in books 1–4 are of necessity simple, and set the target words in contexts familiar to most children. They should be able to focus on the target word without the distraction of an over-stimulating context; for this reason the sentences are low-key in content.

The tests should be dictated to the children. Each child should have a copy of the test and add the missing word as the sentences are read aloud to them.

The practice pages help children to learn the spellings through a variety of activities that are directed towards meaningful repetition of the words. The importance of writing for reinforcing spelling patterns is recognised.

Consistent practice is essential in building up familiarity with frequently occurring patterns and key words. This series will help ensure that children attain competence in spelling at each stage.

Exercise 1

night
right
bright
light
Monday
dinner
supper
butter
farm
farmer

● Write the words.

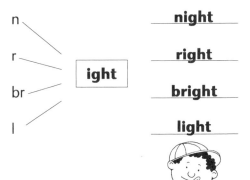

n
r
br
l

ight

night

right

bright

light

● Here is a story with missing words.
Put the words in the right spaces.

supper   Monday   farmer   butter   farm   dinner

Last **Monday** we went to visit a **farm**. We stayed for
breakfast and **dinner**. The **farmer** was milking the
cows. He made some **butter** with the milk. We took the
butter home and put it on our bread at **supper** time.

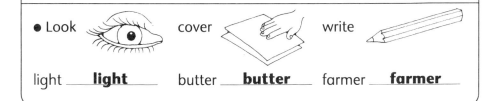

● Look   cover   write

light **light**   butter **butter**   farmer **farmer**

Test 1

- As each line is read to you, write the words in the spaces.

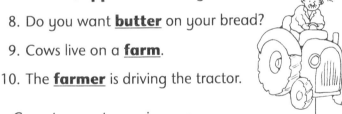

1. We go to sleep at **night**.

2. Is this the **right** way to school?

3. The artist uses **bright** colours.

4. Put the **light** on.

5. I like **Monday** mornings.

6. Put the chairs out for **dinner**.

7. We eat **supper** before we go to bed.

8. Do you want **butter** on your bread?

9. Cows live on a **farm**.

10. The **farmer** is driving the tractor.

- Copy two sentences in your best handwriting.

✓ or ✗	
1.	
2.	
3.	
4.	
5.	
6.	
7.	
8.	
9.	
10.	

SCORE

Practise these:

Exercise 2

rain
again
train
trainers
mother
father
winter
summer
house
mouse

● Write **ai** in the spaces.
Read the words.

r **a** **i** n

ag **a** **i** n

tr **a** **i** n

tr **a** **i** ners

● Finish the pattern.

ai ai ai _____

● There are six words left on the list.
Put them in the right spaces.

It is cold in **winter**. My
mother and **father** like to
stay in the **house** and keep
warm.

In **summer** it is hot.

My little pet **mouse** has to
keep cool.

● Now write the words
in the grid.

● Look   cover   write

summer **summer**   mother **mother**   train **train**

One-a-Week Spelling Tests: Answer Book 2

Test 2

- As each line is read to you, write the words in the spaces.

1. The **rain** stopped our game.

2. Can you show me the picture **again**?

3. The **train** will take us home.

4. Jill can run fast in her new **trainers**.

5. The kitten looked for its **mother**.

6. Ben's **father** gave him a bike.

7. In **winter** we wear gloves.

8. In **summer** we have a holiday.

9. There is an old **house** in our road.

10. We have a pet **mouse** in our class.

- Copy two sentences in your best handwriting.

✓ or ✗	
1.	
2.	
3.	
4.	
5.	
6.	
7.	
8.	
9.	
10.	

SCORE

Practise these:

Exercise 3

face
race
sister
brother
left
eye
baby
other
doing
going

● Look at the list and finish these words.

f **a c e**   go **i n g**

br **o t h e r**   b **a b y**

do **i n g**   r **a c e**

o **t h e r**   e **y e**

● Write words from the word list in the right spaces.

My **b r o t h e r** washed his **f a c e**.

"Where are you **g o i n g**?" I asked.

"I'm going to watch a bike **r a c e**," he said.

"Take your **b a b y** sister," said Mum. "She doesn't want to be **l e f t** at home."

"Oh no," said my brother. "Look what she is **d o i n g**. She is hitting me in the **e y e**."

● Read the passage. There are two words you have not used.

Write them here: _____ **other** _____ **sister** _____

● Look cover write

brother **brother**   eye **eye**   race **race**   left **left**

Test 3

- As each line is read to you, write the words in the spaces.

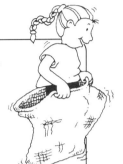

✓ or ✗	
1.	
2.	
3.	
4.	
5.	
6.	
7.	
8.	
9.	
10.	

1. Look at your **face** in the mirror.

2. Carla won the sack **race**.

3. Do you have a big **sister**?

4. I have a younger **brother**.

5. Show me your **left** hand.

6. Keep your **eye** on the ball.

7. The new **baby** is in the cot.

8. Give me the **other** box.

9. What are you **doing** with my book?

10. Are you **going** to the match?

- Copy two sentences in your best handwriting.

SCORE

Practise these:

Exercise 4

tea
teach
teacher
quick
quickly
ticket
kick
thick
spell
spelling

● Finish these patterns.

ea ea ea _____

ick ick ick _____

ell ell ell _____

● Find the three patterns in these words.
Circle the patterns.

(tea)ch t(ick)et qu(ick) (tea)cher k(ick)

qu(ick)ly (tea) sp(ell) th(ick) sp(ell)ing

● Now find all
the words in
this puzzle.

b	s	p	e	l	l	k	t	e	a	j	b	n
q	t	h	i	c	k	p	t	e	a	c	h	x
q	u	i	c	k	l	y	z	x	c	t	d	x
w	g	f	s	p	e	l	l	i	n	g	l	k
l	k	t	e	a	c	h	e	r	m	n	r	l
t	i	c	k	e	t	k	j	h	j	h	g	w
k	i	c	k	b	q	u	i	c	k	b	r	t

● Look   cover   write

quick __**quick**__   tea __**tea**__   spelling __**spelling**__   ticket __**ticket**__

One-a-Week Spelling Tests: Answer Book 2

Test 4

- As each line is read to you, write the words in the spaces.

1. Would you like a cup of **tea**?

2. Can you **teach** me to sing?

3. The **teacher** gave me a new pencil.

4. Be **quick** or you will miss your dinner.

5. The cat ran **quickly** across the garden.

6. You have to buy a **ticket** for the ride.

7. Can you **kick** a ball with your left foot?

8. I like **thick** milk shakes.

9. We can **spell** very well.

10. The **spelling** test is finished.

- Copy two sentences in your best handwriting.

	✓ or ✗
1.	
2.	
3.	
4.	
5.	
6.	
7.	
8.	
9.	
10.	

SCORE

Practise these:

Exercise 5

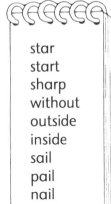

star
start
sharp
without
outside
inside
sail
pail
nail
think

- Look at the list.
  Write **ar** words in the star shape.
  Write **ai** words in the pail shape.

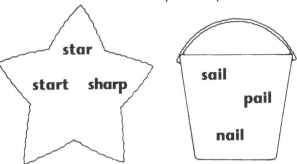

star

start   sharp

sail

pail

nail

- Read the words. Underline the words that are on the list.

"I **think** I'll play **outside** **without** a coat."

"No, it's cold. You must stay **inside**."

- Join the pieces to make three words.

out (side   with (out

in (side

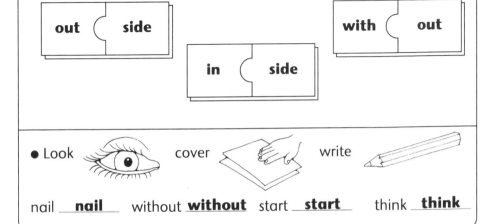

- Look   cover   write

nail **nail**   without **without**   start **start**   think **think**

One-a-Week Spelling Tests: Answer Book 2   © Folens (not copiable)

Test 5

● As each line is read to you, write the words in the spaces.

1. Kim wants to be a pop **star**.

2. We'll **start** when everybody's ready.

3. You need a **sharp** knife to cut fruit.

4. You can go to school **without** a coat.

5. It is warm **outside**.

6. We can stay **inside** the house today.

7. The boat has a blue **sail**.

8. Jack and Jill went to fetch a **pail** of water.

9. Hang your coat on the **nail**.

10. I **think** I know the answers.

● Copy two sentences in your best handwriting.

✓ or ✗	
1.	
2.	
3.	
4.	
5.	
6.	
7.	
8.	
9.	
10.	

SCORE

Practise these:

Exercise 6

garden
bedroom
door
floor
poor
roof
window
yard
leaf
bunch

● Finish writing the labels.

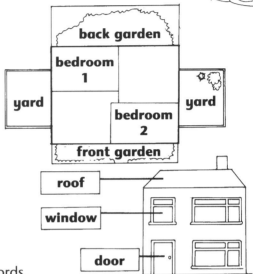

back garden

bedroom 1

yard

bedroom 2

yard

front garden

roof

window

door

● Write the rhyming words.

door   **floor**   **poor**

● Read the sentence.
Find two words from the list. Underline them.

There is only one **<u>leaf</u>** in this **<u>bunch</u>** of flowers.

● Look   cover   write

leaf **leaf** floor **floor** garden **garden** window **window**

Test 6

- As each line is read to you, write the words in the spaces.

✓ or ✗

1. There's an apple tree in our **garden**.

2. Tim has a small **bedroom**.

3. Open the **door** for the teacher.

4. There's paper all over the **floor**.

5. Cinderella looked very **poor**.

6. There is a red chimney on the **roof**.

7. I put a sticker on my **window**.

8. Have you got a back **yard**?

9. The frog sat on a **leaf**.

10. Give Mum a **bunch** of flowers.

	✓ or ✗
1.	
2.	
3.	
4.	
5.	
6.	
7.	
8.	
9.	
10.	

- Copy two sentences in your best handwriting.

SCORE

Practise these:

Exercise 7

town
brown
flower
fold
held
forget
which
doctor
fork
asked

● Write **ow** in the spaces.

t **o w** n   fl **o w** er

br **o w** n

● Finish the pattern.

OW OW OW _____

● There are seven words left on the list.
Find them in this story.
Write them in the boxes.

The doctor held the fork in his hand.

"Do not forget which way to do this," he said.

"Fold back the skin and cut."

"Can I have a bit of the banana?" asked the little girl.

1. **doctor**	2. **held**	3. **fork**
4. **forget**	5. **which**	6. **fold**
7. **asked**		

● Look cover write

flower **flower** forget **forget** which **which** asked **asked**

 One-a-Week Spelling Tests: Answer Book 2   © Folens (not copiable)

Test 7

- As each line is read to you, write the words in the spaces.

1. The shops are in **town**.

2. We have painted our shed **brown**.

3. The clown had a **flower** in his hat.

4. You have to **fold** the paper in half.

5. Gran **held** the baby for a photo.

6. Do not **forget** your swimming kit.

7. I don't know **which** sweet to eat.

8. Go to the **doctor** if you are ill.

9. You need a **fork** to eat spaghetti.

10. Jo **asked** the teacher for help.

- Copy two sentences in your best handwriting.

✓ or ✗
1.
2.
3.
4.
5.
6.
7.
8.
9.
10.

SCORE

Practise these:

Exercise 8

speak
speaking
reading
looking
looked
talk
walk
talking
walked
walking

● Write **ea** in the spaces.

sp e a k   r e a ding   sp e a king

● Write **alk** in the spaces.

t a l k   w a l k   w a l k ed

t a l k ing   w a l k ing

● Write **ing** in the spaces.

speak i n g   talk i n g

walk i n g   read i n g   look i n g

● Write **ed** in the spaces.

look e d   walk e d

● Finish the patterns.

ing ed ing ed ————————————

● Sort the words into families. The first one has been done for you.

~~looking~~   ~~walking~~
~~talk~~   ~~speak~~
~~walked~~   ~~walk~~
~~talking~~   ~~speaking~~
~~looked~~

1	2	3	4
speak	**looked**	**talk**	**walk** **walked**
speaking	**looking**	**talking**	**walking**

● Look cover write

walked **walked** reading **reading** speak **speak** looked **looked**

One-a-Week Spelling Tests: Answer Book 2

Test 8

● As each line is read to you, write
  the words in the spaces.

✓ or ✗

1. Can you **speak** in a loud voice?

2. The queen was **speaking** on television.

3. We have silent **reading** every afternoon.

4. Are you **looking** at the camera?

5. I have **looked** everywhere for my hat.

6. Let me **talk** to your parrot.

7. We can **walk** to the park.

8. Who is **talking** on the telephone?

9. The class **walked** round the old building.

10. The girls are **walking** up the hill.

	✓ or ✗
1.	
2.	
3.	
4.	
5.	
6.	
7.	
8.	
9.	
10.	

● Copy two sentences in your
  best handwriting.

_____

_____

_____

_____

_____

_____

_____

SCORE

Practise these:

Exercise 9

round
ground
found
babies
stories
basket
football
playground
river
come

• Read the sentence.
Write out the words in boxes.

I | found | a | round | coin on the | ground |.

found   **round**   **ground**

• What was the coin?
Clue: it sounds like **found**.   **pound**

• Label the pictures. The words are on the list.

babies   **football**   **basket**   **river**

• Three words are left on the list.
Put them in the right spaces.

The teacher said, "I'll tell you some __stories__ about pets

when you __come__ in from the __playground__."

• Look   cover   write

ground **ground** river __river__ babies **babies** football **football**

One-a-Week Spelling Tests: Answer Book 2

Test 9

- As each line is read to you, write the words in the spaces.

1. Let's walk **round** the school.

2. The apples fell to the **ground**.

3. I **found** your book in my bag.

4. The **babies** are all asleep.

5. Our teacher tells us **stories** every day.

6. We sent a **basket** of flowers for Gran's birthday.

7. Can we play **football** in your garden?

8. Pick up the litter in the **playground**.

9. There is a **river** running through our town.

10. Can you **come** to the shop with me?

- Copy two sentences in your best handwriting.

✓ or ✗	
1.	
2.	
3.	
4.	
5.	
6.	
7.	
8.	
9.	
10.	

SCORE

Practise these:

Exercise 10

happy
funny
sunny
water
table
boy
toy
find
kind
lesson

● Find the rhyming pairs.
Write them on the lines.

sunny	find	boy
toy	funny	kind

| **toy** | **sunny** | **kind** |
| **boy** | **funny** | **find** |

● Read the words.

water   lesson

happy   table

● Write the words in the grid.

w	a	t	e	r	
l	e	s	s	o	n
		h	a	p	p	y
t	a	b	l	e	

● Read and draw:
A funny toy.

A jug of water on a table.

● Look   cover   write

water **water**   kind **kind**   boy **boy**   table **table**

One-a-Week Spelling Tests: Answer Book 2   © Folens (not copiable)

Test 10

- As each line is read to you, write the words in the spaces.

1. Singing makes us **happy**.
2. I think puppets are **funny**.
3. I hope it's **sunny** on our holidays.
4. We have a drink of **water** at dinner time.
5. The dog sleeps under the **table**.
6. There are three girls and a **boy** in my team.
7. I want a **toy** car for my birthday.
8. I'll help you to **find** your lunch box.
9. My brother is always **kind** to animals.
10. Art is my favourite **lesson**.

- Copy two sentences in your best handwriting.

	✓ or ✗
1.	
2.	
3.	
4.	
5.	
6.	
7.	
8.	
9.	
10.	

SCORE

Practise these:

Exercise 11

hair
chair
fair
fairy
apple
fast
last
each
peach
over

- Write **air** in the spaces.

h _a_ _i_ _r_   ch _a_ _i_ _r_

f _a_ _i_ r   f _a_ _i_ _r_ y

- Write **ast** in the spaces.

l _a_ _s_ t   f _a_ _s_ _t_

- Write **ea** in the spaces.

_e_ _a_ ch   p _e_ _a_ ch

- Look at the picture.

Draw a ⬚fairy doll on the ⬚chair.

Give the fairy doll long ⬚hair.

Draw a ⬚peach and an ⬚apple in the bowl.

Draw a pattern all ⬚over the wall.

- Write out the words in boxes.

1. _____**fairy**_____   2. _____**chair**_____   3. _____**hair**_____

4. _____**peach**_____   5. _____**apple**_____   6. _____**over**_____

- Look cover write

each __**each**__   fair __**fair**__   over __**over**__   last __**last**__

Test 11

● As each line is read to you, write the words in the spaces.

	✓ or ✗

1. Comb your **hair** before you go to school.

2. There is a **chair** for everybody in the class.

3. Danny said, "It's not **fair** if I don't win."

4. The **fairy** waved a magic wand.

5. I have an **apple** in my lunch box.

6. You have to run **fast** in the big race.

7. This is the **last** piece of cake.

8. Open the biscuits and give us one **each**.

9. This **peach** is juicy.

10. We can jump **over** this low wall.

1.	
2.	
3.	
4.	
5.	
6.	
7.	
8.	
9.	
10.	

● Copy two sentences in your best handwriting.

SCORE

Practise these:

Exercise 12

girl
bird
first
only
after
year
near
making
letter
home

● Read and draw: A girl near a bird table.
Write the title of the picture below it.

● Read the story.
Write out the words in boxes.

A [girl] got some [bird] food to put in the garden. At [first] [only]
one bird came, but [after] a [year] the garden was full of birds.

"I'm [making] a bird table," wrote the girl in a [letter] to her
friend. "I'll put it [near] the window. When I am at [home] I can
watch the birds all day."

1. **girl**   2. **bird**   3. **first**   4. **only**   5. **after**

6. **year**   7. **making**   8. **letter**   9. **near**   10. **home**

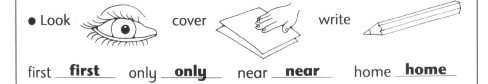

● Look   cover   write

first **first**   only **only**   near **near**   home **home**

Test 12

- As each line is read to you, write the words in the spaces.

1. Let the new **girl** play with us.
2. The big **bird** made a nest on the school roof.
3. I want to be **first** in the line.
4. There is **only** one place left on the bus.
5. Come to my house **after** the match.
6. We go on a trip every **year**.
7. Don't stand **near** the road.
8. We are **making** models of houses.
9. Write a **letter** to your pen-friend.
10. You must be **home** by five o'clock.

- Copy two sentences in your best handwriting.

✓ or ✗	
1.	
2.	
3.	
4.	
5.	
6.	
7.	
8.	
9.	
10.	

SCORE

Practise these:

Exercise 13

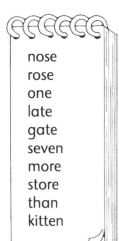

nose
rose
one
late
gate
seven
more
store
than
kitten

● Sort the words into three boxes.

| ˙nose | late | more |
| gate | store | rose |

| gate | |
| late | Both words have | ate |.
| **nose** | |
| **rose** | Both words have | ose |.
| **store** | |
| **more** | Both words have | ore |.

● Read the sentences.
Write the words in boxes.

I can see | more | than | one | kitten | in the box. There are | seven |
kittens.

1. __more__   2. __than__   3. __one__   4. __kitten__   5. __seven__

● Draw and write.

A nose smelling a rose.

● Look   cover   write

rose __rose__   gate __gate__   more __more__   one __one__

One-a-Week Spelling Tests: Answer Book 2   © Folens (not copiable)

Test 13

- As each line is read to you, write the words in the spaces.

✓ or ✗

1. The cat has a pink **nose**.

2. There is a red **rose** in the vase.

3. Give me **one** of those apples.

4. Do not go to bed **late**.

5. Please close the **gate** after you.

6. There are **seven** candles on the cake.

7. You can have some **more** lemonade.

8. We can **store** the paper in a cupboard.

9. Seven is one more **than** six.

10. I would like a **kitten** as a pet.

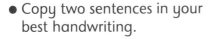

	✓ or ✗
1.	
2.	
3.	
4.	
5.	
6.	
7.	
8.	
9.	
10.	

- Copy two sentences in your best handwriting.

SCORE

Practise these:

Exercise 14

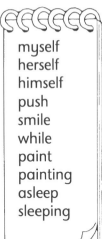

myself
herself
himself
push
smile
while
paint
painting
asleep
sleeping

● Make five of the words on the list by drawing a line to the correct ending.

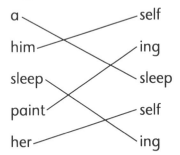

a ———— self
him ———— ing
sleep ———— sleep
paint ———— self
her ———— ing

● Finish the words in the boxes.

p **u** s **h**	w **h** **i** **l** **e**	s **m** **i** **l** **e**	p **a** **i** n **t**
p u **s** **h**	**w** h **i** **l** **e**	s m **i** **l** **e**	**p** a **i** n **t**
p u **s** **h**	**w** h i **l** **e**	**s** m **i** **l** **e**	**p** a **i** n t
p **u** **s** h	**w** **h** i **l** **e**	**s** m **i** **l** e	**p** a **i** n **t**
	w **h** **i** **l** e	**s** **m** **i** **l** e	**p** a **i** n t

● Write the words in the right spaces.

1. The joke made us ___**smile**___.

2. Can you ___**paint**___ the gate red?

3. Wait for a little ___**while**___.

4. Give the car a ___**push**___ to make it start.

 ● Look   cover   write

asleep **asleep** painting **painting** herself **herself** while ___**while**___

One-a-Week Spelling Tests: Answer Book 2   © Folens (not copiable)

Test 14

- As each line is read to you, write the words in the spaces.

1. I went to the cinema by **myself**.
2. Jane washed **herself** with the yellow soap.
3. Tom fell but he picked **himself** up again.
4. You can **push** the swing and make it go high.
5. I like to make the baby **smile**.
6. Let the porridge cool for a **while**.
7. The **paint** is still wet.
8. The artist was **painting** a picture.
9. The cat fell **asleep** on the bed.
10. You are **sleeping** at your friend's house tonight.

- Copy two sentences in your best handwriting.

✓ or ✗	
1.	
2.	
3.	
4.	
5.	
6.	
7.	
8.	
9.	
10.	

SCORE

Practise these:

Exercise 15

bee
free
queen
lake
bake
spoon
meet
street
week
three

• Look at the list.
Write the words with **ee**.

bee	**free**
queen	**meet**
street	**week**
three	

• Write the words with **ake**.

lake	**bake**

• Write the word that is left over.

spoon

• Write **ee** words in the right spaces.

1. I shall m __eet__ you at the end of our s __treet__ .

2. The q __ueen__ b __ee__ is very big.

3. This w __eek__ we can have t __hree__
   f __ree__ ice creams in our shop.

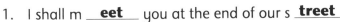

• Look cover write

spoon __spoon__ bake __bake__ lake __lake__ street __street__

One-a-Week Spelling Tests: Answer Book 2

Test 15

- As each line is read to you, write the words in the spaces.

1. The **bee** is looking for flowers.

2. The cakes are **free** if you buy some coffee.

3. The **queen** wore a gold crown.

4. The **lake** is deep and blue.

5. On Tuesdays we **bake** biscuits.

6. Eat your soup with a **spoon**.

7. You must **meet** us at four o'clock.

8. There are ten houses in our **street**.

9. We have a spelling test every **week**.

10. You have **three** minutes to finish the sums.

	✓ or ✗
1.	
2.	
3.	
4.	
5.	
6.	
7.	
8.	
9.	
10.	

- Copy two sentences in your best handwriting.

SCORE

Practise these:

Exercise 16

frog
frost
cave
wave
save
shell
smell
dive
drive
driver

- Look at the list.
  Sort the words into the boxes.

frog frost	cave wave save	shell smell	dive drive driver
These words have fr	These words have ave	These words have ell	These words have ive

- Read the meanings. Write the words.

A small animal   **frog**

A dark hole in rocks   **cove**

Jump into the water   **dive**

- Read the sentences. Write the words in boxes.

  We went to the beach. I found a shell . I could smell the
  sea in it. I could hear a wave roaring in it.

  "Let's dive into the sea," said Dad. "You can save your
  shell and take it home."

1. **shell**   2. **smell**   3. **wave**   4. **dive**   5. **save**

- Look   cover   write

driver **driver**   frost **frost**   smell **smell**   save **save**

One-a-Week Spelling Tests: Answer Book 2   © Folens (not copiable)

Test 16

- As each line is read to you, write the words in the spaces.

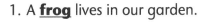

1. A **frog** lives in our garden.

2. The windows are covered with **frost**.

3. There's a **cave** in the rocks by the sea.

4. You have to **wave** goodbye to Gran.

5. We can **save** some money for the holidays.

6. The snail has a **shell** on its back.

7. The **smell** of cooking makes me hungry.

8. Katy can **dive** in from the side of the pool.

9. We went for a **drive** in the country.

10. The train **driver** saw the red signal.

- Copy two sentences in your best handwriting.

✓ or ✗	
1.	
2.	
3.	
4.	
5.	
6.	
7.	
8.	
9.	
10.	

SCORE

Practise these:

Exercise 17

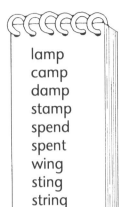

lamp
camp
damp
stamp
spend
spent
wing
sting
string
swing

- Look at the list. Write the rhyming words.

lamp **camp** **damp** **stamp**

wing **sting** **string** **swing**

- Finish the patterns.

amp amp _____

ing ing _____

- Label the pictures.

  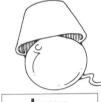

| **wing** | **stamp** | **swing** | **lamp** |

- Read the sentences. Write the words in boxes.

1. "What did you | spend | your money on?"
   "I | spent | it on a pen."

2. The tent in our | camp | was | damp |.

3. Tie the | string | on to the balloon.

1. **spend**   2. **spent**   3. **camp**   4. **damp**   5. **string**

- Look cover write

spend **spend**   wing **wing**   string **string**   stamp **stamp**

One-a-Week Spelling Tests: Answer Book 2   © Folens (not copiable)

Test 17

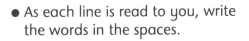

- As each line is read to you, write the words in the spaces.

	✓ or ✗
1.	
2.	
3.	
4.	
5.	
6.	
7.	
8.	
9.	
10.	

1. Buy a new front **lamp** for your bike.

2. We are going to **camp** in our tent.

3. The carpet was **damp** after the flood.

4. You must not **stamp** your feet as you walk in.

5. Everybody can bring some money to **spend**.

6. Harry **spent** all his money on books.

7. The bird slept with its head under its **wing**.

8. Some insects can **sting** you.

9. Pull the **string** to make the kite fly.

10. We all ran to play on the **swing**.

- Copy two sentences in your best handwriting.

SCORE

Practise these:

Exercise 18

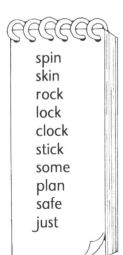

spin
skin
rock
lock
clock
stick
some
plan
safe
just

● Look at the list.
Write the words that end with **in**.

_____**spin**_____   _____**skin**_____

● Write the words that end with **ck**.

_____**rock**_____   _____**lock**_____

_____**clock**_____   _____**stick**_____

● Read the sentences. Circle the words
from the list. Write the words in the box.

The robbers wanted (some) money.

They met at five o'(clock).

They made a (plan).

"We can take the (lock) off
the (safe)," said one robber.

They opened the (safe).

"There's nothing here," said
the robber.

"(Just) a (rock) and (some) dust."

● Look 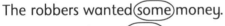   cover   write

stick **stick**   plan _**plan**_   spin _**spin**_   clock _**clock**_

Test 18

- As each line is read to you, write the words in the spaces.

	✓ or ✗
1.	
2.	
3.	
4.	
5.	
6.	
7.	
8.	
9.	
10.	

1. The skater can **spin** round on the ice.

2. The man slipped on a banana **skin**.

3. Let's sit on a **rock** and watch the sea.

4. Remember to **lock** the door.

5. Your **clock** is five minutes fast.

6. Get the glue and **stick** the picture on to the card.

7. Put **some** sandwiches in your bag.

8. Make a **plan** of the classroom.

9. Keep your money in a **safe** place.

10. Ben has **just** been to the dentist.

- Copy two sentences in your best handwriting.

SCORE

Practise these:

Exercise 19

skipping
getting
biggest
any
anything
many
before
belong
their
two

● Read the words. Find three word families.
Write them in the boxes.

got   skipping   getting   biggest
skip   bigger   get   skipped
big

got get getting	skipping skip skipped	biggest bigger big

● Circle **any** in these words.

(any)thing   m(any)   (any)where   (any)one

● Put the words in the right spaces.

two	their	before	belong

1. The letter A comes __**before**__ the letter C in the alphabet.

2. "Does this book __**belong**__ to you, Peter?" asked the teacher.

3. The children put __**their**__ coats on and went home.

4. Most people have __**two**__ ears.

● Look cover write

skipping __**skipping**__ getting __**getting**__ biggest __**biggest**__ their __**their**__

Test 19

• As each line is read to you, write the words in the spaces.

1. Let's play with the **skipping** rope.

2. I'm **getting** a new computer game.

3. Sam has the **biggest** balloon.

4. Are there **any** more people for dinner?

5. I don't want **anything** to eat today.

6. How **many** children are there in the school?

7. I'm **before** you in the line.

8. These rulers **belong** to our class.

9. The children put **their** coats on.

10. Give me **two** biscuits.

	✓ or ✗
1.	
2.	
3.	
4.	
5.	
6.	
7.	
8.	
9.	
10.	

• Copy two sentences in your best handwriting.

_____

_____

_____

_____

_____

_____

SCORE

Practise these:

Exercise 20

number
television
use
ruler
catch
match
September
November
lamb
thumb

● Look at the list.
Write all the words with **mb**.

number	**September**
November	**lamb**
thumb	

● Circle **use** in the words below.

am(use)   ref(use)   exc(use)

● Cross out the words you do not need.

Make sure you catch/~~match~~ the ball in the ~~catch~~/match tonight.

● Read the meanings.
Write the words.

● Draw a lamb on television.

We watch it ___ **television**

We measure with it ___ **ruler**

A young animal ___ **lamb**

The 11th month ___ **November**

It's on your hand ___ **thumb**

We use it to count ___ **number**

● Look   cover   write

television **television**   use **use**   catch **catch**   lamb **lamb**

Test 20

- As each line is read to you, write the words in the spaces.

	✓ or ✗
1.	
2.	
3.	
4.	
5.	
6.	
7.	
8.	
9.	
10.	

1. What **number** is your house?

2. I watch **television** after tea.

3. We **use** boxes to make models.

4. The **ruler** is one metre long.

5. Try to **catch** the ball.

6. You have to **match** the word to the picture.

7. School starts in **September**.

8. The weather is cold in **November**.

9. The sheep looked for the lost **lamb**.

10. Tom hit his **thumb** with the hammer.

- Copy two sentences in your best handwriting.

_____

_____

_____

_____

_____

_____

SCORE

Practise these:

Exercise 21

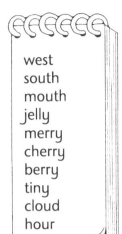

west
south
mouth
jelly
merry
cherry
berry
tiny
cloud
hour

● Write the words that rhyme with these.

merry ___**cherry**___   ___**berry**___

mouth ___**south**___

● Write **ou** in the spaces.

cl **o u** d   s **o u** th

h **o u** r   m **o u** th

● Read the words. Write them into the grid.

jelly   hour   cloud   south
merry   tiny   berry   mouth

● Look   cover   write

cherry ___**cherry**___ south ___**south**___ hour ___**hour**___ west ___**west**___

Test 21

● As each line is read to you, write the words in the spaces.

	✓ or ✗
1.	
2.	
3.	
4.	
5.	
6.	
7.	
8.	
9.	
10.	

1. The sun sets in the **west**.

2. In winter the birds fly **south**.

3. The hippo has a big **mouth**.

4. We had **jelly** at the party.

5. We sang a song called, "We wish you a **merry** Christmas".

6. The **cherry** tree has pink blossom.

7. This holly has one red **berry**.

8. The insect is **tiny**.

9. A **cloud** is covering the sun.

10. We learned spellings for an **hour** today.

● Copy two sentences in your best handwriting.

_____

_____

_____

_____

_____

_____

SCORE

Practise these:

Exercise 22

children
storm
wheelchair
market
corner
fear
clear
world
ready
slow

● Look at the list.
Find and write:

Words with **ch**:

___**children**___ ___**wheelchair**___

Words with **ea**:

___**fear**___ ___**clear**___ ___**ready**___

Words with **r** as the third letter:

___**market**___ ___**corner**___ ___**world**___

Words beginning with **s**:

___**storm**___ ___**slow**___

● Find all the
words in this
puzzle.
Colour them
yellow.

j	s	l	o	w	c	x	f	e	a	r	b
w	o	r	l	d	z	d	c	l	e	a	r
p	w	h	e	e	l	c	h	a	i	r	r
x	s	t	o	r	m	z	r	e	a	d	y
j	l	k	c	h	i	l	d	r	e	n	w
k	j	m	h	c	o	r	n	e	r	y	t
n	m	d	f	v	m	a	r	k	e	t	g

● Look   cover   write

storm **storm** corner **corner** wheelchair **wheelchair**

One-a-Week Spelling Tests: Answer Book 2   © Folens (not copiable)

Test 22

● As each line is read to you, write
  the words in the spaces.

1. There are thirty **children** in our class.

2. Do not go out in the **storm**.

3. Jackie put pop star stickers on
   her **wheelchair**.

4. We can buy fruit at the **market**.

5. The room has a lamp in each **corner**.

6. Red Riding Hood has no **fear** of wolves.

7. You can cross when the road is **clear**.

8. The **world** is round.

9. Are you **ready** for school?

10. The bus is too **slow**.

● Copy two sentences in your
  best handwriting.

✓ or ✗
1.
2.
3.
4.
5.
6.
7.
8.
9.
10.

SCORE

Practise these:

How well did I do?

Shade in your test scores on this graph.

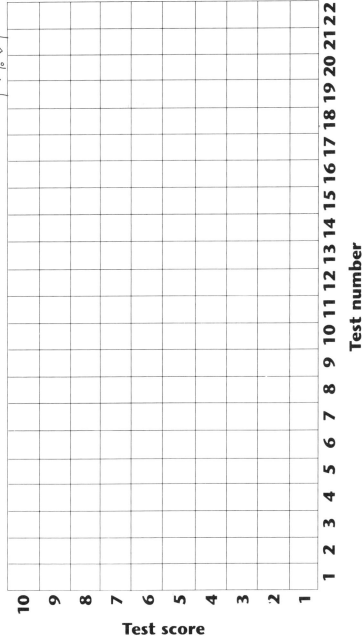

Test score

10 9 8 7 6 5 4 3 2 1

Test number

1 2 3 4 5 6 7 8 9 10 11 12 13 14 15 16 17 18 19 20 21 22

One-a-Week Spelling Tests: Answer Book 2